IT'S TIME TO EAT TACO SALAD

It's Time to Eat TACO SALAD

Walter the Educator

Silent King Books
A WhichHead Entertainment Imprint

Copyright © 2024 by Walter the Educator

All rights reserved. No part of this book may be reproduced in any manner whatsoever without written per- mission except in the case of brief quotations embodied in critical articles and reviews.

First Printing, 2024

Disclaimer

This book is a literary work; the story is not about specific persons, locations, situations, and/or circumstances unless mentioned in a historical context. Any resemblance to real persons, locations, situations, and/or circumstances is coincidental. This book is for entertainment and informational purposes only. The author and publisher offer this information without warranties expressed or implied. No matter the grounds, neither the author nor the publisher will be accountable for any losses, injuries, or other damages caused by the reader's use of this book. The use of this book acknowledges an understanding and acceptance of this disclaimer.

It's Time to Eat TACO SALAD is a collectible early learning book by Walter the Educator suitable for all ages belonging to Walter the Educator's Time to Eat Book Series. Collect more books at WaltertheEducator.com

USE THE EXTRA SPACE TO TAKE NOTES AND DOCUMENT YOUR MEMORIES

TACO SALAD

It's time to eat, the table is set,

It's Time to Eat

Taco Salad

A meal is coming you'll never forget.

Taco salad, crunchy and bright,

With colors and flavors that feel just right.

Lettuce so crisp, a green little boat,

Holding the toppings to help it float.

Tomatoes so red, juicy and round,

Adding a sweetness that's world-renowned.

Beans so soft, packed with power,

Giving us strength hour by hour.

Cheese is next, it's yellow and fun,

Melty and tasty for everyone.

Sprinkle some chips, hear the loud crunch,

Perfect to nibble on with your lunch.

A dollop of salsa, spicy and bold,

Bringing some heat when the weather is cold.

It's Time to Eat

Taco Salad

Avocado slices, creamy and sweet,

Make the salad feel like a tasty treat.

Add sour cream, a little white swirl,

For every boy and every girl.

Mix it together, give it a spin,

Now the taco salad fun can begin!

Each bite is a party, a flavor parade,

A yummy creation that we just made.

Scoops and scoops, we gobble away,

Filling our bellies for the rest of the day.

Eating together, it's such a delight,

Sharing a meal that feels just right.

So next time you're hungry, don't make a fuss,

Taco salad's ready, just waiting for us.

A dish so simple, a meal so neat,

It's Time to Eat

Taco Salad

Taco salad time can't be beat!

It's fun to help and join the prep,

Layering goodness step by step.

A family feast, with hands all around,

Building a salad that's truly renowned.

Now let's all cheer, a loud hooray,

For taco salad to save the day!

Healthy and tasty, it's quite a feat,

It's Time to Eat

Taco Salad

A dish that's both fun and good to eat!

ABOUT THE CREATOR

Walter the Educator is one of the pseudonyms for Walter Anderson. Formally educated in Chemistry, Business, and Education, he is an educator, an author, a diverse entrepreneur, and he is the son of a disabled war veteran.
"Walter the Educator" shares his time between educating and creating. He holds interests and owns several creative projects that entertain, enlighten, enhance, and educate, hoping to inspire and motivate you. Follow, find new works, and stay up to date with Walter the Educator™

at WaltertheEducator.com

www.ingramcontent.com/pod-product-compliance
Lightning Source LLC
LaVergne TN
LVHW052016060526
838201LV00059B/4044